For George, with all my love
JP

For teachers and educators everywhere.
Thanks for making learning a hoot!
MF

Text copyright © 2020 by Jane Porter
Illustrations copyright © 2020 by Maddie Frost

First US edition 2021

Library of Congress Catalog Card Number pending
ISBN 978-1-5362-1521-2

20 21 22 23 24 25 LEO 10 9 8 7 6 5 4 3 2 1

Printed in Heshan, Guangdong, China

This book was typeset in Zalderdash.
The illustrations were done in mixed media.

Candlewick Press
99 Dover Street
Somerville, Massachusetts 02144

www.candlewick.com

CANDLEWICK PRESS

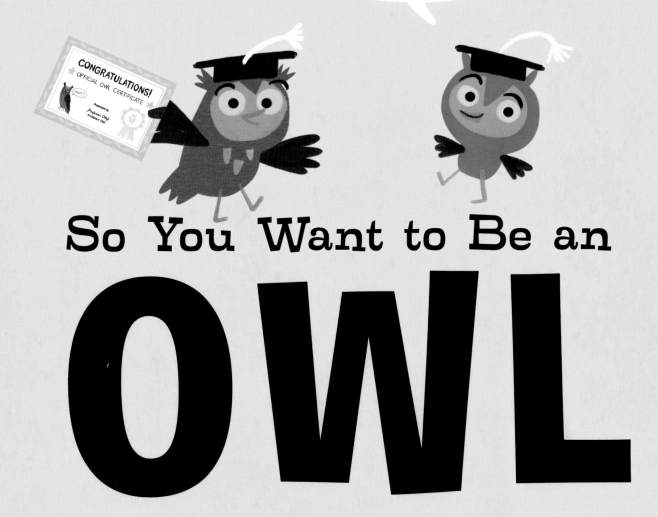

Yes, please!

So You Want to Be an

OWL

JANE PORTER illustrated by **MADDIE FROST**

Welcome to Owl School!

I'm Professor Olaf, and I'm here to teach you all about being an owl. We're always on the lookout for sharp-eared, keen-eyed, silent types to join Team Owl.

THE OWL CODE:

Be alert

Be watchful

Be silent (shh!)

ALL ABOUT OWLS

MORE ABOUT OWLS

LOTS MORE ABOUT OWLS

Professor Olaf

Let's take a look at the checklist:

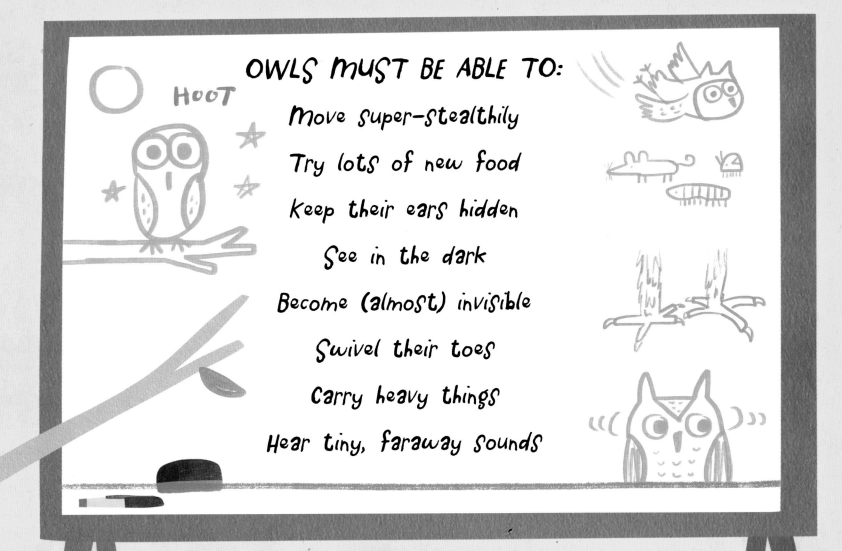

OWLS MUST BE ABLE TO:

Move super-stealthily

Try lots of new food

Keep their ears hidden

See in the dark

Become (almost) invisible

Swivel their toes

Carry heavy things

Hear tiny, faraway sounds

HOOT

Do you think it looks easy?
Get your feathers straight, and we'll get started!

Before we begin . . .

Let's take a look at you. Hmm. You are rather LARGE for an owl. Even my biggest cousin, Blakiston's Fish Owl, is only as heavy as a small cat, and my smallest relative, the Elf Owl, doesn't weigh more than a heaping tablespoon of sugar.

Blakiston's Fish Owl

Elf Owl

Are YOU heavier than a cat?
I thought so. . . . And I see you have no feathers!
This is going to be a LONG day.
Still, we'll see what we can do with you.

Being a good owl is all about SILENCE and STEALTH.

Oh, and wisdom (that's another way of saying we're pretty smart).

We owls are special, you see.

If you're going to join us, you'll have to live by our strict code:

Be alert! Be watchful! Be silent!

Got your pencil case? Come on!

All the other trainee owls are ready,
and I can hear the hoot for lesson one. . . .

LESSON ONE: Can you fly?

Have you learned to fly yet? No? Humans are such late developers. I started flying when I was just a couple of months old. You need to get yourself some of these:

Big wings help us to glide slowly and save energy.

A fringe on our feathers muffles sound so we can fly silently.

6

Owl feathers aren't waterproof, so we don't like to go out in the rain (except for our cousins the Little Owls—they don't mind getting wet).

Can YOU fly silently? Go on—give it a try.
Oh dear, that's just embarrassing.
Well, if you can't fly, let's see if you can at least blend in. . . .

You can't see me, can you?

LESSON TWO:
Can you disappear?

We owls are masters of disguise. Our feathers match the places we live, making us almost invisible. Many of us sleep during the day, so keeping well hidden is vital.

Eastern Screech Owl

Some of us are mottled like tree bark . . .

Burrowing Owl

or dusty like the ground . . .

Snowy Owl

or white as snow.

Believe it or not, smaller birds don't like us very much and sometimes attack us because they are worried we'll hurt them—another reason to keep hidden.

Can you hide? Growing some feathers would be a start. Well, if camouflage isn't for you, how good are you at spotting things? Let's take a look at your eyes. . . .

LESSON THREE: Can you see in the dark?

Am I making you feel uncomfortable? Sorry! Owls are famous for staring. Our eyes are very special—and very large. They take up 70 percent of the space in our skull.

The color of our eyes shows when we like to hunt:

daytime   dusk and dawn   night

We can't roll our eyes like you, but we can turn our head 270 degrees— that's nearly all the way around! We've got twice as many bones in our neck as you have.

Our eyes are tube-shaped, which makes them more sensitive to light and movement, but we can't see much color.

Now, can you blink for me? Don't forget your other eyelids. You've only got ONE that moves for each eye? We have THREE: one for sleeping, one for blinking, and one for keeping our eyes clean.

blinking

cleaning

sleeping

How far can you turn your head? Is that all? I am starting to feel quite sorry for you humans. In addition to eyesight, another one of our senses is very important. Time to listen up!

LESSON FOUR:
How's your hearing?

Owls are excellent listeners. (We're always alert, and we only sleep deeply for eleven seconds at a time.) We keep our ears hidden under our feathers, so they are top secret. Those tufty things some owls have on top of their heads are not ears—we use them to show how we're feeling. Many of us have one ear higher than the other, which means we can tell exactly where each sound is coming from.

Not ears

Real ears are here . . .

and here.

Our faces are shaped like a satellite dish to funnel sounds to our ears. This can magnify what we hear up to TEN TIMES!

Noise

Noise

LESSON FIVE:
Can you catch your own dinner?

Our super-sharp eyes, tip-top hearing, and high-tech feathers are for one thing only: HUNTING. We can spot our prey up to half a mile away. See it, hear it, swoop in—that's our motto.

Our feet are very special. We can move one of our toes on each foot, so that two toes are pointing forward and two are going backward, for extra grip. That's called being ZYGODACTYL. (I told you we were smart.)

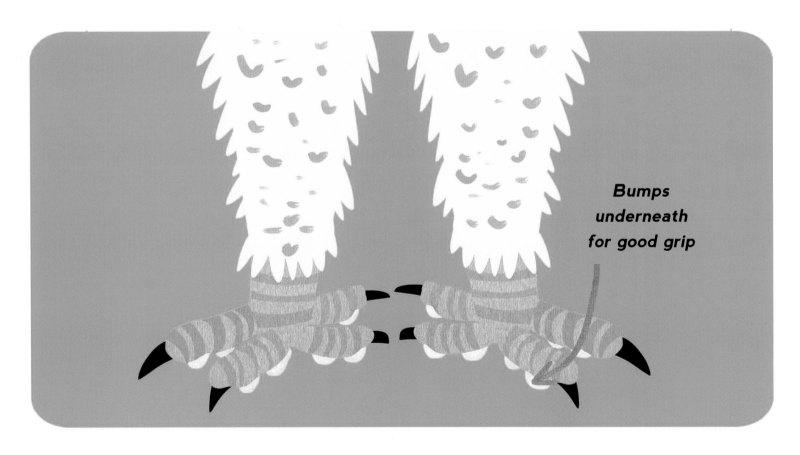

Bumps underneath for good grip

Our special feet help us to carry things that are very heavy. Great Horned Owls can carry FOUR TIMES their own weight. Razor-sharp talons make sure that we don't drop anything.

Let's take a look at your feet. How much do you think YOU could carry with them? Have you just cut your toenails? BIG mistake. Anyway, all this talk of hunting is making me hungry. It must be lunchtime.

Owl Café

Fresh mouse

Cucumber sandwiches

Crunchy beetles

Moth mousse

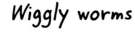
Wiggly worms

Snails in sauce

Centipede surprise

Chocolate ice cream

LESSON SIX:
Can you swallow a mouse whole?

Owl table manners are—ahem—a little different from human ones. We don't waste time chewing! We swallow our food down whole, and we eat a LOT—Barn Owls eat about 1,000 mice a year, but some of us prefer insects, fish, or even rabbits.

Most of these sound delicious. Which ones would YOU choose?

After a good meal, don't you just love to cough up
all the bones and fur? No?

Ah, I can see we need to talk about
owl pellets. If you ever see an owl coughing, it's probably
making an owl pellet. We can't digest bones or fur or feathers,
so we make them into packets and spit them out. Scientists love
looking at them to learn all our owl secrets.

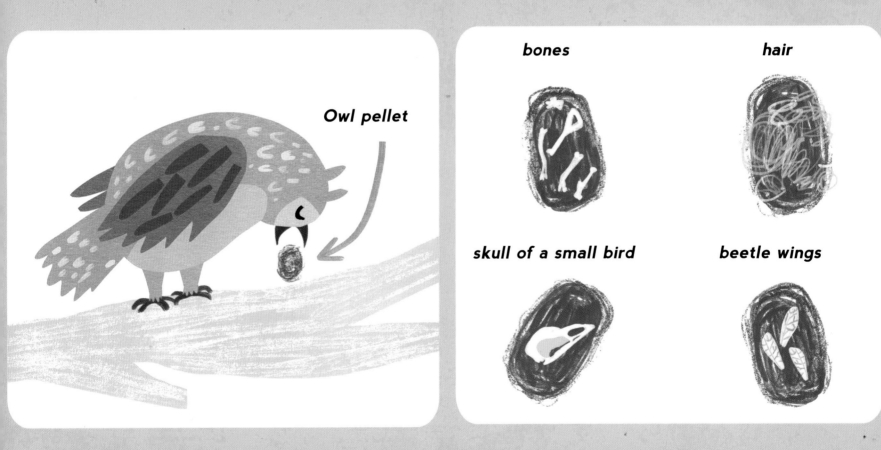

Owl pellet

bones

hair

skull of a small bird

beetle wings

Have I made you feel a bit queasy? Oh dear.
Better move on to something VERY important. . . .

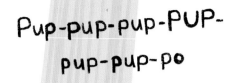

Pup-pup-pup-PUP-pup-pup-po

Spectacled Owl

Woof woof!

Barking Owl

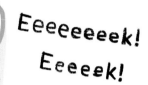

Eeeeeeeek!
Eeeeek!

Barn Owl

LESSON SEVEN: How's your hooting?

Whi whi whi whi whi whi WHI!

Peruvian Pygmy Owl

Everyone knows that owls say "twit-twoo," don't they? Wrong! It's only Tawny Owls who do that, and the sound is actually made by *two* owls calling to each other. Some of us also hiss, bark, screech, whistle, rattle, snore, or growl. Why do we do it? To show where we live, to find a friend, and to scare enemies.

Oop! OOP!

Long-Eared Owl

Boo-BOOK!

Boobook Owl

Hoo-hoo-hoo-hooooo

Great Horned Owl

Peep peep! Peep!

Mountain Scops Owl

Hoo! Hoo! Hurry up!

Can you make any of these sounds?
Give it a try!
LOUDER! You need other owls to hear you
from half a mile away. That's better. Just
two lessons left. Time to follow me
to a place I'm very fond of . . .

19

LESSON EIGHT:

Can you live in a tree?

It's nice to come home to a warm roost after a hard day at Owl School. Welcome to my house!

Cozy, isn't it? Other birds rush around collecting twigs to build nests, but not us owls. We look for a suitable hole in a tree and move right in.

We don't all live in trees. One of my relatives, the tiny Elf Owl, lives in a cactus in the desert.

And can you guess where the Burrowing Owl lives? In a hole in the ground! (Usually one made by someone else.)

Where would you make YOUR nest? Up high or down low? Would it be prickly or soft? Hold on—how rude of me! I have forgotten to introduce you to someone very important.

LESSON NINE:
Can you raise chicks?

This is my mate, Ottilie! You might have noticed that she's larger than me. Female owls usually are. Each year clever Ottilie lays a clutch of beautiful, almost round eggs.

Darling, you've done it again!

And about a month later, the eggs hatch into little owlets.

Owlets might look cute, but they are a lot of work. We need to feed them TEN times a day. And we have to protect them. Anyone who comes near should fear our talons. It's hard work being a parent.

Now that you know what it takes to be an owl, would
you still like to join us? You're not the best I've ever
seen, but you've tried hard, so I'm making
you an honorary member of Team Owl.

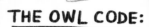

THE OWL CODE:
Be alert
Be watchful
Be silent (Shh!)

ALL ABOUT OWLS

MORE ABOUT OWLS
LOADS MORE ABOUT OWLS

Professor Olaf

25

Welcome to Team Owl!
Congratulations!

Just hoot if you need me, and don't forget:

Be alert!   Be watchful!   Be silent!